MW01289009

Monkeys For Kids

Amazing Animal Books for Young Readers

by John Davidson and Annalee Davidson

~~~

Smashwords Edition

Read More Amazing Animal Books

Table of Contents

1. Fascinating Facts about Monkeys

Here are few fascinating facts about monkeys!

1. Monkeys peel their bananas before eating them.

2. The word monkey means curious and mischievously behaving animal.

A golden lion tamarin monkey (Leontopithecus rosalia)

3. Most monkeys have a pouch in their cheek used to store food. This way they can gather food extremely fast, and chew and swallow it later.

4. Monkeys grab using their fingers AND toes.

5. Monkeys spend most of their time resting, over 80% of its lifetime.

6. Howls from monkeys can be heard from two miles away in the forest and over three miles in the open.

7. The Mirikina monkey live in South America, it makes such horrible noises at, the natives nick-named it the "devil monkey."

8. The Red Colobus monkeys, are hunted by man and chimpanzees, for food.

9. Titim monkeys in South America are the most romantic monkeys. They have only have one life-long mate. Titim monkeys have been seen together holding hands, cuddling, and twisting their tails together. These monkeys also can become very worried, if they are not together.

10. Capuchins monkeys or ringtails have many useful skills. They use rocks to crack open nuts in order to eat what is inside. They will rub caterpillars against a branch to remove its hair, before eating it. Ringtails also use branches from the forest to cub snakes to death.

11. Squirrel monkeys have over twenty sounds that are unique only to them.

12. Monkeys were one the most popular animals, they have been seen in paintings on the walls of caves and used in rock art.

13. In the ancient civilizations of China, India, Egypt, and Greece monkeys were considered symbolic, as they represented human beings.

14. Monkeys have adapted over thousands of years here are some of the changes:

Old World Monkeys	New World Monkeys
Only Active during the day	Over 10 species are nocturnal, only active at night
Sitting pads on their bums	No sitting pads
32 teeth	36 teeth
96 species of monkeys	187 species of monkeys (as of 2009)
Non – Prehensile Tail, used only for balance	Prehensile tail, used for swinging and grabbing objects

2. Where Monkeys Live

You may have seen monkeys in a zoo, but what is their natural habitat, or home? Monkeys usually are found in warm countries of the world which include South America, Asia, Africa, and Europe.

Scimmie © fragolerosse - Fotolia.com

Some monkeys live primarily in trees, while others live mainly on the ground. The ground monkeys have more organized rules than the tree monkeys.

Howler and Capuchin monkeys (ringtails) are found in South America. They travel in big troops of around 5 to 20 in number.

Macaque monkeys are found primarily in India, but can be seen in the South Pacific Islands and Burma.

Baboons, the Black Ape, and the Mandrill monkey are located in Africa.

Closeup of a baby Japanese macaque (Macaca fuscata)

3. What Monkeys Eat

Monkeys eat all kinds of fruits, veggies, leaves, small insects, and nuts. They prefer to eat natural and fresh food. This is why monkeys are seen in large numbers in tropical rain forest, mountains, and on islands.

Depending on where the monkey lives tells us the certain foods they may eat. For example, monkeys living in southern India have plenty of bananas and coconuts to eat. Spider monkeys live mainly in the rainforests of South America, eating ripe fruit and green tree leaves. They also have a great liking for eggs, especially from birds or reptiles. Gorillas, which live mainly on the ground, enjoy ants and termites. Baboons seen in thick forests are meat eaters. They hunt for rabbits and birds, it is also believed, and if given the opportunity; baboons will feast on baby chimpanzees!

Monkey hugging cat © OlegD - Fotolia.com

It's quite common to see all types of monkeys eating bugs from each other's fur. It is their way of keeping clean.

Many monkeys have pouches in their cheeks which are used to store food. This is rather helpful when they are on the run and do not have time to chew before the next bite. They can store the food, and then later, in a safe place, the monkey can chew and swallow the food.

Young male proboscis monkey on Borneo Island in Malaysia

4. Pet Monkeys

Having a pet monkey is becoming more popular. Monkeys are small enough to fit into a backpack, making it a desirable pet. They are also known to be very playful animals, again another perk to a pet monkey. Unfortunately, laws on certain areas make it impossible to have a monkey for a pet.

pet baby monkey © meisterphotos - Fotolia.com

Monkeys are very adorable animal and having one as a pet may seem fun. But before buying one there are some factors which need to be considered. First, make sure there is not a law forbidding pet monkeys in your state. It would be rather sad to find this fact out, just a little too late. There may also be rules and regulations that go along with owning an exotic monkey, as a pet.

If it is legal to own a pet monkey, then you can proceed with considering other important factors. Next a pet monkey, as with a wild monkey, needs a comfortable environment. The environment needs to have enough space for the monkey to move around freely. The exact size of cage will depend on the type and size you choose as a pet. It should also include toys for them to play with. Thirdly, your pet monkey will need plenty of food to keep them active and healthy. In the last section you read about what monkeys eat. Fourth, make sure to research to find if there is a good vet nearby that is an expert in handling monkeys. Last, Along with many other factors, make sure you are prepared for the responsibly that comes with having any type of pet.

If you are sure you want a pet monkey, the most recommended as a pet is the capuchin monkey. These are found in the North and South America. Capuchin monkeys have a great endearment for others (monkey and humans, alike). They weight around 3 to 9 pounds, a very lean and agile monkey. These monkeys have fur ranging in color from light tan to cream.

Another monkey commonly raised as pets is a monkey found in the rain forest, the Marmoset monkey. However, they are not easily trained or domesticated. They are wild animals, they tend to be very wild, dangerous, and spastic once they grow up. Many people that do choose to raise these monkeys do so in large groups in a wild habitat. It includes a dominant female and dominant male monkey. This family setting is made to control their behavior so that they do not act wildly.

An interesting fact about monkeys raised in these habitats, is the smaller monkeys that the human chooses to bottle-fed, is very unlikely to one day be capable of feeding their young. This is because they themselves were not cared for naturally, so they did not learn how to take care of their offspring in such a way.

One more time, before buying any pet, but especially a monkey, do lots of research online and in books to know all about the care of pet monkeys.

5. Species of Monkeys

Monkeys are primate mammals that can be found throughout the World. They belong to the same scientific family as that of human beings. Monkeys have tails of different sizes that are very different from apes. Monkeys generally have high intelligence and are quick learners. There are various species of monkeys found throughout the World.

Monkeys can be generally divided into two groups based on their origin. The species of monkeys found in Southern and Central America are called New World Primates, while those found in Asia and Africa are known as Old World Primates. At this time more than 260 species of monkeys are known to exist throughout the World. The most commonly found species are Capuchin monkeys, the Rhesus Macaque, and the Grivet. Albert, the first monkey to be sent to space, was a monkey belonging to the Rhesus species. Able and Miss Baker, Rhesus Macaque monkeys, were the first monkeys to return to Earth after a successful space trip.

White-faced capuchin monkey on coconut tree, national park of Cahuita, Caribbean, Costa Rica.

Some popular species of monkeys belonging to the New World category are Pygmy Marmosets, Golden Lion Tamarin, Emperor Tamarin, and Owl monkey. The Pygmy Marmosets are the smallest known species, they measure about half of a human finger when they are born. They like to eat the sap from the trees found in the rainforests of South America. The Golden Lion Tamarin has golden hairs sprouting from all over its body, that is why it is known as the Golden Lion. The Emperor Tamarin has an easy to spot, white beard. The Owl Monkey, as the name says, looks like an owl with no wings.

A few examples of Old World monkeys include the species Mandrill, Golden Snub-Nosed monkeys, Spectacled Langur, and Roloway monkey. The Mandrill has a very long red nose bordered with white fur. The Golden Snub-Nosed monkeys have golden hairs on that cover the head. They can survive in cold arctic temperatures due to the thick fur covering. Golden Snub-Nosed monkeys also survive on lichens, small plants that grow on trees, and tree bark. Spectacled Langur has circular white patches around its eyes that look like spectacles, or glasses. Langur are the largest of all monkey species. Lastly, the Roloway monkey has a completely white haired body including the eyebrows with a completely black face.

Chimpanzee with a cub on mangrove branches.

6. Endangered Monkeys

All monkeys like to live in forests where they get their food and have shelter. Due to the destruction of many forests in the World, monkeys are becoming endangered. Another reason that there is an increasing number of endangered monkeys, is poaching. Monkey's skin is used for many different purposes.

The following is a list of endangered monkeys found in different parts of the world.

1.Roloway Monkey -

It is found in West Africa, in the country of Ghana and along the Ivory Coast .They are hunted by human beings for commercial meat, causing them to be endangered.

2. Pennant`s Red Colobus -

These monkeys are found in Equatorial Guinea in the Bioko Island in West Africa. They are endangered monkeys due to their bush meat. Most hunters hunt them for meat which is popular in the island. There are special reserves set up in the Island to protect them but the poachers still manage to kill them.

3. Tana River Red Colobus/Mangabev -

They are found in Kenya located in East Africa. These monkeys are becoming extinct due to the destruction of their habitats, by clearing of forests for farming purposes.

4. Kipunji

This monkey is found in Tanzania in East Africa. They are mainly endangered by the clearing of trees where they live and hunting activities in the area.

5. Pig-tailed langur

Pig-tailed langurs are found in Indonesia in the Mentawai Islands .They are affected greatly by tree logging in their area, which threatens their existence.

6. Golden Headed Langur

This species of langurs is found in Vietnam. They were greatly hunted for traditional medicine in Vietnam, threatening to make them extinct. The government of Vietnam has put policies in place to try and protect their survival.

7. West Purple-faced Langur

Found in Sri Lanka, the west purple-faced langur is endangered due to the declining growth of forests in this region.

Common Langur monkey found in India.

8. Grey-shanked Douc monkey

The grey-shanked douc monkey is found in Vietnam. Due to illegal expansion of agriculture and tree logging their habitats are declining. They are also hunted which makes them fall under the category of endangered monkeys.

Black and White Colobus (Colobus guereza) Resting

7. Rain Forest Monkeys

Most of the monkeys found in the Amazon rainforest have one common trait, their prehistoric tails! They are used to wrap around tree branches, it acts as a 5th limb.

Some of the most common Amazon rain forest monkeys are marmosets, capuchins, spider monkeys, howler monkeys, tamarins and squirrel monkeys.

Scientists are continually finding new species of monkeys in the Amazon Rain Forest. In early 2009, in a remote part of Brazil, scientists found a brand new species of rain forest monkey, it is called the Mura's Tamarin. The Mura's Tamarin monkeys are considered endangered, due to tremendous amount of logging, which is destroying their natural habitat. Continual efforts are being made to save this species of tamarins from becoming extinct.

Pied tamarin, Saguinus bicolor, 4 years old © Eric Isselée - Fotolia.com

Marmosets are often used as pets, even though they are a very wild rainforest monkey. To read more on the Marmoset monkey refer to the section on pet monkeys.

Spider monkeys are an amazing rain forest monkey, and they are called so because they have very long prehensile tails, legs and arms. Among all the rain forest monkeys, this species is considered to be the most intelligent one.

8. Baby Monkeys

Baby monkeys are the newborn babies of monkeys. They are usually small when they are born, weighing between 2 – 4 pounds. Some of them are so small they can be held in the palm of your hands. Baby monkeys are often playful, they mostly enjoy playing with their mothers, jumping from one tree to the next. Babies are usually closer to their mothers and like being cuddled by them. Baby monkeys usually feed on their mother breast milk since they are still too young to feed on anything else; they are mammals, just like humans.

9. Small Monkeys

One of the smallest monkeys is called the baby pygmy. This monkey is so small it can wrap itself around a finger and finger can still be seen! The baby pygmy is between 4.5 and 6 inches tall and only weighs 3 to 5 ounces.

Pygmy Monkey Pygmy Marmoset (5 weeks) - Callithrix (Cebuella) pygmaea

© Eric Isselée - Fotolia.com

10. Howler Monkeys

One of the most common species of monkeys is the howler monkey. They are distinct because of their loud howls. They can be heard up to a distance of over 3 miles (5 km) away. Howler monkeys, are the second loudest animal on Earth after the blue whale.

Mantled howler (Alouatta seniculus) resting

© michaklootwijk - Fotolia.com

They live in tall trees. Mostly they are found in the regions of South and Central America. The canopy of the rain forest in countries such as Brazil in the Southern part, Northern Argentina, Bolivia, and Paraguay forms homes for many of these types of monkeys.

They live in groups ranging from 4 to 19 members. They are mostly active during the day moving from one tree top to the other in search of food. They spend most nights sleeping. The life span of these monkeys is about twenty years.

They are strict vegetarians. They eat food originating from plants such as flowers, leaves, and fruits from the trees. In places such as Belize there is a law protecting people from destroying the trees from which the monkeys get their special foods.

Most adult howlers are black and brown in color. The young and the females are mostly lighter in color. Mature howlers can grow up to a height of 4 feet and have a body weight of about 8 to 22 pounds .They usually have a tail which is long, a short snout ,and round nostrils. The female howlers usually bear one child at a time.

A major threat to the howler monkey is the destruction of their habitats by humans cutting down the forests. Another threat is they are hunted for food by some native tribes. Lastly, their exportation as pets also endangers their existence.

11. Marmoset Monkeys

Marmoset monkeys are a type of monkeys that can be turned into one of the most amazing pets in the world, as you read earlier. They are quite small, a marmoset monkey is about twenty centimeters (3/5 of a foot) long. Most of them can live up to twenty years. They belong to the group of animals known as primates which are considered to be very intelligent animals. These particular monkeys have unique features as compared to other types of monkeys. One of these features is that they have claws instead of nails. Also other monkeys have wisdom teeth but marmoset monkeys lack them.

Black and white Marmoset monkey on a branch

Keeping this cute monkey as a pet is simple. All you have to do is understand what the monkey needs in order to live, eat well, and also be happy. To make a tiny living place for the monkey just requires a minimum cage size which allows the pet space to move about a little. A space that is too small makes them bored and definitely unhappy.

Letting the monkey out for some time for it to exercise is a practice that is healthy. The marmoset monkey eats greens and fruits. It is encouraged to give them a source of protein such as insects. As long as they are well taken care of with the right food and cage, these monkeys are the best of pets. Their personality is great. They are not only intelligent but also affectionate and very playful.

In order to allow them to move about freely in the home, these monkeys need to be in a house that has been baby-proofed to avoid messing things up. Also, they should be sprayed to keep away the heavy scent they have from their urine and poop. This is because they like marking their territory, as a dog may do, leaving the heavy scent all over your home.

12. Snow Monkey

Snow monkeys get their name because they like the snow and live in places that are covered with snow about 1/3 of the year.

Japanese Snow Monkey © SeanPavonePhoto - Fotolia.com

Snow monkeys are from northern Japan. Their real name is the Japanese Macaque, snow monkey is a type of nickname. They love snow and they can survive winter temperatures of -15° C (5° F). Just imagine you living in your refrigerator freezer; this is how the snow monkey can lives for a good portion of the year.

They are medium size monkeys, covered with brown-gray fur. During the winter their fur grows very thick, however during the summer when it is warmer their fur is lighter. Their face and hands, on the bottom, are red, and their tail is short. A full grown monkey can have a length of 2.5 – 3 feet (80 - 95 cm); the male weight ranges from 22-30 lbs (10 to 14 kg) and a females weighs around 12 pounds (5.5 kg).

Snow monkeys eat many different varieties of food. They eat things like: seeds, fruits, insects, berries, leave, invertebrate (like worms), tree bark, and bird eggs.

They are like kids when it is time to have fun. They like to play, swim, and even roll snowballs and throw at to each other. Another fun fact about snow monkeys is that they use all four legs to get around, but if they are holding something, then they will use their hind legs (their two bottom legs).

13. Spider Monkeys

Spider monkeys are one of the biggest and smartest monkeys. They have very thick fur, long arms, legs, and tails. They live in the rain forest high in the tops of the trees where they swing around using their tails. They are really fast and can swing with their tails without falling. They eat fruit, nuts, bird eggs, leaves, flowers, and bugs. They like fruit the best, but have to eat bugs when there is no fruit. Spider monkeys like to have lots of friends and live with lots of other spider monkeys. They live with 35 or more other monkeys.

Geoffroy's Spider Monkey, Black-handed Spider Monkey

They make different sounds when communicating with each other. They have their own language. One sound they make sounds a lot like a dog barking. They also make weird crying sounds and they scream a lot.

Spider monkeys can live to be about 22 years old, weigh about 13 pounds, and can get up to 6 feet tall. They don't have thumbs like people but they don't have a hard time grabbing things with their fingers.

Since people are cutting down trees in the rain forest, spider monkeys are endangered.

14. Capuchin Monkeys

Capuchin monkeys are native to South and Central America. They are small, and very demanding. They are intelligent beings that can grow to 12-22 inches and weigh 3 pounds. Their average life span is 40 years, so those who to plan on raising a capuchin monkey need to make a long-term commitment and have patience.

Capuchin White Faced Monkey

© snaptify - Fotolia.com

The following are some tips to raise a baby Capuchin monkey. The first things you need to make sure is if it is legal to own this exotic pet. Baby capuchins need a large strong cage that is minimum of 6 feet high and 4 feet in width. Have two cages, one for the indoors and one for the outdoor. They need to be supervised at all times. So when you are away from home place them in the cage.

The capuchin monkey's cage should be equipped with many branches that it can climb on and should also have entertainment items like swings, toys, ladders, pipes, tires, etc. Also, a sleeping box needs to be placed inside the cage so that it can rest in it.

Capuchins need to eat a healthy diet. Buy special primate diets in the pet stores that are available in the form of dry powder. You can also feed baby food to it. You need to feed baby capuchins once every 2 hours.

Your capuchin monkeys need to be cleaned and washed every day. Use mild baby shampoos.

When you let the capuchins out of the cage put diapers on them to prevent messes and accidents everywhere in the house. When it grows a little older toilet train it. Capuchins need a lot of love and affection. Play with it often and give your undivided attention to it. Create a bond between yourself and the capuchin to make it listen to you. Train the capuchin to obey your commands. Repeat its name regularly while feeding it and playing with it. Praise it when it responds to its name. Teach the monkey small commands like sit, stand, come, go, etc. Reward it whenever it obeys your command.

When you have visitors at home keep the capuchin locked in its cage as they can be fearful when they are vulnerable. As it gets older and more socialized you can let them interact with the visitors.

Take your capuchin to your veterinarian regularly for health checkups and get them vaccinated.

15. Squirrel Monkeys

Squirrel monkeys can be found in South and Central America. They like to live in tropical forest jungles especially close to any kind of flowing water. There are actually five species of these monkeys they are: the Common, the Black-Capped, the Central American, the Golden-Backed, and the Black-Headed. They all look alike except for the little differences on the color of their fur, and the places that they live. They are called squirrel monkeys because their size and color, looks like a squirrel, also, they spend most of their time in trees.

These are very small monkeys that measure less than one foot to be exact, 25 cm from top of their head to the beginning of their tail. Their tail is longer than their body, measuring 14 to 19 inches, and their weight range from one to three pounds. Squirrel monkeys have short olive and grey fur, with yellow legs a white face.

Squirrel monkeys like to eat small animals, insects, buds, nuts, plants, flowers, and fruits. However, they don't like to eat leaves. With their great eyesight, they can see from far away a bright color flower for their next meal.

Young Squirrel Monkey <u>squirrel monkey</u>

© Eric Gevaert - Fotolia.com

These monkeys do not have a prehensile tail meaning that they cannot use their tail to hold onto tree branches like other monkeys do. They use their tail to help them balance when climbing on high places. Another fun fact about the squirrel monkeys is that they have nails instead of claws. Also, it is fun to know that compared to their body size, their brain is the largest, if you compared them with other monkeys.

Because squirrel monkeys are so smart and small, people have kept them as their pet. To find out more about these monkeys or any from this book, ask your parents to help you search online to learn more interesting facts about the squirrel monkeys.

We hope you have enjoyed learning about monkeys. If you want to learn more amazing things about other animals, read one of the other books in the series **Amazing Animal Books** at our website.

<u>monkey faace</u> © Darren Nickerson - Fotolia.com

Read More Amazing Animal Books

http://AmazingAnimalBooks.com

Join our newsletter and receive

Amazing Animal Fact Sheets and

Get new books to review as soon as they come out

Newsletter Sign Up at http://AmazingAnimalBooks.com

Like us on Facebook

https://www.facebook.com/pages/Amazing-Animal-Books/392591680849107#

This book is published by

JD-Biz Corp

P O Box 374

Mendon, Utah 84325

http://www.jd-biz.com/

Made in the USA
Columbia, SC
03 December 2021

50189251R10024